lobster   shrimp   crab   crayfish

waves   boats   seagulls   fish

 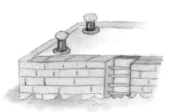  

anchor   quay   boat   lighthouse

net   fish   fishermen   crates

Camdean Nursery

Published in the UK in 1994 by Schofield & Sims Limited, Huddersfield, England.

0 7217 5025 7

PLAY WORDS

At the Seaside

SCHOFIELD & SIMS LIMITED, HUDDERSFIELD, ENGLAND

waves

boats

seagulls

fish

The sea

The is calm and the

are gently rocked by the  .

In the sky above the ,

fly round and round crying noisily.

Sometimes, they dive to catch the

 in the . When there

is a storm, the  can capsize

the  .

bather　　　　parasol　　　　beach-ball　　　　sandcastle

The beach

In summer, children play happily all day on the  . They can play with a  , make a  and dig channels. Mummy relaxes nearby, sitting under a  . She watches the  jumping in and out of the waves. In winter, the  is empty.

seaweed

shells

crab

starfish

The rocks

Walking among the ⬤ when the tide is out is lots of fun. You can find and collect 🐚 by looking amongst the 🌿. Between the ⬤ , there are rock pools. There you can sometimes find ⭐ . Watch out! – under the 🌿 there may be a little 🦀 which can nip!

lobster

shrimp

crab

crayfish

Shellfish

There are lots of shellfish in the sea. The is the most fun because it walks sideways! It has claws, but the has the biggest claws. The looks like a very large . The , the , the , and the all have hard shells.

fins

scales

eggs

shark

Fish

 move under the water using

their . The bodies of the

are covered in . There are

many types of  in the sea, but

they all try to hide when the fierce

 swims past.  lay

from which hatch baby fish.

net

fish

fishermen

crates

The trawler

The is a fishing boat. Behind it, it tows a big to catch . When the is full, the pull it in. They put the  in . In the evening, the sails back to port. The unload the .

anchor

quay

boat

lighthouse

The harbour

There are lots of in the . Some have dropped on the seabed and the others are neatly moored along the . When fishing has finished, the sailors unload their . At night, the guides the and marks the entrance to the .

flippers   mask   cylinders   diving-suit

Divers

 swim underwater. They wear

a  because the water is cold.

To breathe,  carry two

of oxygen. They swim slowly by

flapping long . To see clearly

under the water, wear a

.

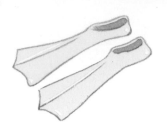

flippers

mask

cylinders

diving-suit

bather

parasol

beach-ball

sandcastle

seaweed

shells

crab

starfish

fins

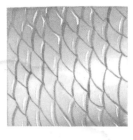

scales

eggs

shark